THE MELODY LINGERS

New and Selected Poems of Shlomo Vinner

Revised edition

Translated by

Howard Schwartz

Harold Ellason

Laya Firestone-Seghi

Edited by Howard Schwartz

Singing Bone Press

2023

ACKNOWLEDGMENTS

Translations of some of these poems have previously appeared in the following journals: *Arc, Centerpoint, The Charlton Review, Midstream, Rubicon, Sagarin, Seven Gates, Shirim, Watermark, Webster Review* and *Writ*.

Some poems were also included in *Lyrics and Laments: Selected Translations from Hebrew and Yiddish* by Howard Schwartz (Kansas City: BkMk Press, 1979).

A selection of these poems also appeared in the anthology *Voices Within the Ark: The Modern Jewish Poets* (New York: Avon Books, 1980).

Poems Copyright © 1976, 1986, 1990, 2014, 2019, 2022 by Shlomo Vinner

Translations Copyright © 1976, 1987, 1988, 1989, 1990, 2019, 2022 by Laya Firestone-Seghi, Howard Schwartz, and Harold Ellason

Cover illustration Copyright © by Yitzhak Greenfield 2019 All Rights Reserved

The first edition of this book was published by Singing Bone Press in 2019.

Library of Congress Control Number: 2018963459

Vinner, Shlomo

[Selections. English. 2019]

The Melody Lingers: New and Selected Poems of Shlomo Vinner / translated by Harold Ellason, Laya Firestone-Seghi, and Howard Schwartz; edited by Howard Schwartz
Translations from Hebrew — second edition, revised

ISBN 978-0-933439-17-7
1. Jerusalem—Poetry. 2. Vinner, Shlomo—Translations, English.
I. Schwartz, Howard. II. Firestone-Seghi, Laya. III. Ellason, Harold.
IV. Title.
© 2019, 2023 by Shlomo Vinner
All Rights Reserved

                Singing Bone Press

For Hava, Yael, and Noa

I thank the three translators—Harold Ellason, Laya Firestone-Seghi, and Howard Schwartz—for their huge endeavor in translating my poems. I could not have hoped for a better result.

Shlomo Vinner

CONTENTS

FOR A FEW HOURS ONLY

Jerusalem 1

Midnight and Ten Minutes 2

Again Rain 4

Death in the Sea 5

Erev Rosh Hashana 6

In the Closet 8

Evening in the Hospital 9

Training on the Shore 10

Autumn Maneuver 11

The Tired Light Descends 14

The Need to Love 15

The Evening Is Ours 18

Parting 21

JERUSALEM AS SHE IS

From My Father I Inherited 25

Mount of Olives 28

Cancer Ward 33

Jerusalem as She Is 38

Aquarium 45

Life Goes On 48

In the Children's Room 50

Hidden Love 53

A Visit to the Old School 61

Syllables 65

The Error 66

The Evil Spirit 68

The Plagues 69

Church 70

Seasonal Wind 71

Real Life 72

Sabbath Eve 74

Jet Lag 76

The View 77

An Evening Jog 78

Directing the Traffic 80

Tour Guide 82

Overnight on the Lakeshore 83

FROM THIS DAY OF YOM KIPPUR TO THE NEXT

From This Day of Yom Kippur to the Next 87

THE MELODY LINGERS

1985—Visit 113

Is This Old Age? 118

The Melody Lingers 125

A Child with Special Needs 126

On the Twenty-First of Tishrei 128

The Sun at Its Peak 129

I Hear 130

Navigation 131

Night Thoughts 132

Sleeping Problems 134

Pictures at an Exhibition—The Museum of Modern Art 137

In His Hand 138

The Taste of Life 139

Playground 140

Birthday Song 142

On Hudson River's Bank 144

The Last Quartet 145

The Melody Remains 146

Departure 149

The Poet 151

The Translators 153

FOR A FEW HOURS ONLY

JERUSALEM

Jerusalem,
the former address of God;
sometimes
they still imagine His silences
between walls and bells.
To hear His heart
they call to Him over loudspeakers
and wait until everything dissolves.

When the smoke clears, the burnt house
and the bodies of the beloved
are revealed.

The hearts of old trees are heavy as stone;
longings that last too long
turn into thorns in the valley;
dreams are exchanged
for piles of rusted scrap.

At the end of the wars,
amid new signs and arrows,
the birds leap on grass:
Jerusalem 1967,
the former address of God.

L. F.-S. and H. S.

MIDNIGHT AND TEN MINUTES

1.

Because of deep depression and a sudden urge,
a star threw itself
from the seventh heaven.
We mourn for it,
but who will mourn
for us?

2.

The moon under cover of planes
sets out on a routine mission.
If it doesn't detect us,
we will be able to stay
another day at most.
Or else, we shall be forced to uproot ourselves,
and to camouflage our love
with sand.

3.

Midnight and ten minutes,
and what else?
The anthem was played,
the clock set for seven exactly,
the stars remained without reason.

The angels' wings are artificial, dusty.

They lie in deep trenches.

Soot hides the light on their faces.

Only a blanket still covers our love.

And the hours pass over us in silence.

L. F.-S. and H. S.

AGAIN RAIN

Again rain
forces the cyclamens to blossom
and us to continue the game
of love and separation.
Whoever does not die in it
must come back to play again
as in a bullfight,
sometimes with a torn heart,
sometimes with crushed limbs.

A quiet evening descends on the crowd
cheering from the sidelines.

In the morning
I get up,
write *need*,
but think *pain*.
Rain is poured on the earth like water
on the face of one tortured,
whose tormenters wait for him to revive
so they can continue.

We thought to rest—
but again rain,
again rain
forcing the cyclamens.

L. F.-S. and H. S.

DEATH IN THE SEA

The sea took him to itself,
filled his mouth with water,
left him little to speak of himself,
left his friends to speak of him
in praise.
The sand has its conjectures
and all its patience
for the sea.
At the end
it will all be revealed.
But we cannot wait.
We must gather what is given,
gather and go.

Banners, lanterns, and spades.

Behind us
only the seaweed,
the crabs dead in the sand,
can testify
how the sea took him.

L. F.-S. and H. S.

EREV ROSH HASHANA

1.

Like this, without a moon and far from spring,

God hurts us with his thoughts.

Rams' horns that have long been silent

will cry out and again be silent.

Dry leaves will tremble.

The wind will rouse the world

to prepare for the coming.

And only the clouds passing above know

of the lines in the palm of God's hand,

and how our fate is written in them

in the dark

and far from spring.

2.

I anticipate more hardships.

The troops are ready,

said the commander at the end of the big maneuver.

A bird shall carry the voice.

Whoever is not able will fall and be left behind.

The time approaches.

A shiver passes through the pines,

white dust awakens.

Not far from here,

on the sea,

the wind rests

like military planes on the ground.

But it is ready.

It waits for a sign.

I anticipate more hardships.

3.

The world has a birthday

we celebrate without it.

Without it we make blessings over the bread

and the years.

We expect the tumult to stop for a moment

so we can hear its heart.

Evening will come.

Our eyes will adjust to the dark

and the dark to our eyes,

our faces to the pain

and the pain to our faces.

It is the world's birthday.

L. F.-S. and H. S.

IN THE CLOSET

Still playing:
God locks me in a closet
along with the key.
I grope in the dark and breathe the scent
of strange loves. Blindly I must wait,
but I know,
even if He lingers,
He will not come.

They covered His death
with artificial roses,
concealed His bones,
scattered leaves where there were trenches,
set up angels, chiseled faces
that would not hurt the stone too much.

The dust of ruins settles in my lungs.
The key is in my hand.

L. F.-S. and H. S.

EVENING IN THE HOSPITAL

Evening. Again a nurse by the window.
Her bright hair unbridled.
It is doubtful there will be time
to think of this again come night.

Even the roses on the table
will not hold on forever.
The evening, like a girl in love,
will pick a petal and still another.
The scent of another world blows through
the open window.
But the patient cannot recall it,
wrapped in a blanket
along with the dream of his friends,
their sickness and their death—
his face to the wall, his back to the world.

L. F.-S. and H. S.

TRAINING ON THE SHORE

Children

they teach to walk,

soldiers

to crawl.

And between one lesson and another

they are shown the sand

God showed Abraham

when He made him a nation

wandering like sand.

They are shown the moon-struck sea,

grass sprouting from the hearts of stones

that once were the wall of a temple.

And at midnight

dew rises from the beloved land,

swearing-in whispers.

The stars swear-in the grass,

the grass—the stars.

Children they teach to walk,

soldiers—to fall.

L. F.-S. and H. S.

AUTUMN MANEUVER

1.

Summer falls

and grief grows long

as shadow of mountains.

In the fields autumn crocuses will grow

and longings and weeds.

Summer falls.

2.

Soldiers.

Early in the morning

with faces grey as olive tree trunks,

grief nailed in their hearts

like tacks in their soles.

In the evening

lying down on the hard earth,

scattered in the field like mounds of dirt.

Their bodies cover the hushed sprouting of the grass

and the sighs of thorns on the slope of the mountain.

3.

The end of summer,

and the faces of the soldiers

are drawn with thoughts of bayonets and girls.

At the entrance to the city,

facing olives which wave their arms,

crowded together in six trucks,

they sing.

In the field they practiced their death and the fall,

left their dreams behind in one of the pits

beside the burnt vehicle.

At the entrance to the city

in six trucks

they are singing.

4.

Only whitewashed stones

remain as reminders an army camped here.

In the circle a flag was raised and lowered;

in the rectangles sweating men

lay side by side.

Next to an olive tree with a hollow trunk,

very close to the border,

they dug ditches to lie in.

The grass exalted above them to the clouds,

in their eyes a handful of dust.

Only the whitewashed stones remain.

And grief grows long

as shadow of mountains.

L. F.-S. and H. S.

THE TIRED LIGHT DESCENDS

The tired light descends and will descend further

to the sea overflowing like a girl's

breasts full

of the desire to love

soft as thighs

offering no resistance

like the sand

into which we sink

as into old pain

and we are here

for a few hours only

on sand that can still be counted

and minutes later

facing stars that cannot

though it is hard to understand how

the tired light descends

and will descend

further

L. F.-S. and H. S.

THE NEED TO LOVE

> *Therefore shall a man leave his father and mother, and shall cleave to his wife; and they shall be one flesh.*
>
> Genesis 2:24

The need to love is the need to leave and move on.

So it is. Distant towers.

Giant letters of an announcement stuck in the clouds.

Buzzing of words in the electric air.

Pillars. Pillars.

The sweet sighs of the poplars in the wind.

Above all

the sudden whistle of twenty sirens

announces an impending disaster.

If we put an ear to the evening

as to a seashell

it can still be heard.

The need to love is the need to think

of all one must leave and move on.

Thus, years grow thick in pines.

In us too time calms down

like rain in dark cisterns.

Leaves' shivering in wind's fingers.

Preparations of ants in the loose dirt.

Death is mentioned in pseudonyms
in chats of low bushes, in the doctors' report,
signed on the trunks of olive trees—
their branches shaking.
And what we cannot name
will be lost forever,
until its loss is no longer remembered
or we lose our memory.

And the ability to love is the ability to leave
and move on.
Fall will return for the tired trees.
God will put them to sleep
like a patient in dangerous surgery.
Thorns will die.
The earth will give a final answer to those who search.
But the grass persists,
perhaps out of habit,
perhaps out of desire that cannot be measured.
And see
how words cannot explain, so
you must understand, without words,
how to distinguish between sand and sand,
sand and sea,
our silence and the world,
how to be stirred by what is stirred in me

when I say

the evening grows dark in us, crying,

and death passes,

or when I say

the ability to love is the ability to leave

and move on.

L. F.-S. and H. S.

THE EVENING IS OURS

1.
Unlike me,
the sun has lost its strength.
It peeks behind the mountain
like a boy standing on his toes,
peeking over a fence.
Lying among the bushes.
The grass murmurs like a rumor.
The world kindles its lights
that emerge from inside like oranges
from the darkness of the tree.
I clench my fists.
The evening is still ahead.

2.
The evening is ours.
In the fig trees
heavy and ancient thoughts pass through the branches
like the murmur of pupils
calculating ninety-six times ninety-six
and God knows.
Memories of the moment grow in us as in trunks
so serious in the tangle of love and leaves

that we are ready to remain covered

by deepening shade

if only we are not held to account.

3.

Yet already

behind the mountain

the world spells out our fate

in the language of ciphers and signs.

The alert watchtower

translates dim lights

into the language of daily dangers,

directions, intentions.

The spotlights betray the lovers in the grass,

on the sand.

Wandering jackals are revealed.

The wind gathers its data

and returns.

Our fate is whispered from mouth to mouth,

leaf to leaf,

in the language of ciphers and signs,

in the language of the sea,

in the language of the stars.

4.

In the darkness the landscape

is a ghostly ship,

a city of dim lights, thoughts

like branches stumbled on unexpectedly.

I hear voices singing,

their faces hidden

in the bushes,

in the grass.

Chimes pour out their hours one by one,

flooding the sleeping cities

wave after wave.

L. F.-S. and H. S.

PARTING

1.

A sword of light is unsheathed from a cloud,
a sign
for the doves and the evening
and the scaffold left by a building.
Jerusalem besieged between walls
sets free the bells
and the dark birds above us.
Among thorns, the crocus will blossom,
without warning, without leaves,
but it is doubtful
that we can do the same.
And on your forehead
the sign of parting is drawn,
concealed behind your hair.

2.

We must do everything now.
It's doubtful we'll be in love
next summer.
Your hair will grow;
the wind will blow it like a sail
wandering eternally
with clouds and wind,
sand and birds.

Those standing
like pillars of a house in ruins,
will be broken by the prolonged standing.
We shall have to move on
or separate.
Between now and then
evening descends,
the air trembles,
and the sea floods the sand
with white shells, murmurings,
garbled syllables, memories,
and doubts
we will love again.

3.
Our love's left
like a sailboat in winter.
The waves erase
the traces of our feet in the sand.
And look,
the riverbeds
have filled.
Dead leaves float in them.
On the bank,
visions of an autumn evening
grow wild.

L. F.-S. and H. S

JERUSALEM AS SHE IS

FROM MY FATHER I INHERITED

1.
From my father I inherited
the headache,
the backache
and the heartache.
When it aches
I remember him
with love.
There is no better way to remind me
I am with him.

He is with me.

2.
I don't know if I saw him on the street
or in a dream.
For a dream
he was too real.
On the other hand
not real enough.
He had the smile of someone who knows a secret
he's not supposed to know.
I ignored it
and returned
a smile that meant something else.

Once again he had his beard
and I wanted to ask
since when.
But I kept silent.
I thought:
Why should I,
maybe it's just a dream.

3.
In the calm summer nights
of Jerusalem
I recall my father's heart attack.
God pinched his heart,
like a father who pinches his son.
On one hand,
it is meant to express love;
on the other—
to hurt.
Perhaps not even on the other?
I mean—
the same hand.

4.
The door slamming in my dream,
on a rusted hinge, in the darkness,
is the door death opened

when my father became sick
and didn't close.

The door slamming
in the darkness,
on a rusted hinge,
in my dream
will never close.

5.
And furthermore,
my father's gestures
remain in me.
Sometimes his voice
speaks from my throat,
sometimes—the sighs.
The heavy stone
on his heart
is now on his grave.
And on my heart—
my stone.

H. S.

MOUNT OF OLIVES

In memory of Yehuda Yaari

1.

The Mount of Olives—
a huge ship in dry harbor waiting to sail
to the resurrection of the dead.
Sometimes the wait is long.
First the sea must return
and flood the mountains.
But at times
it seems that it will set sail very soon.
I awaken in panic:
Wait a second for me too,
I'm already coming.

2. *A Painless Death*
He laid the next day's clothes on the chair.
The house was in order,
which was a relief.
Fully fatigued, he turned on
the boiler and lay down to rest. He would
shower later.
When he fell asleep, he had no idea
that his heart would stop in a few minutes.
From his position in bed, he also didn't know

when it stopped.

I never saw him sleep so peacefully, his wife declared.

A wave of gentleness flooded her and urged her to kiss him.

She brought her lips to his forehead.

Only then she noticed he was not

alive. Dead.

A painless death.

3.

Now and then I think I feel like someone

about to die.

How does someone about to die feel?

How does someone

not about to die feel?

How do

I feel?

Thank you very much!

And you?

4.

Recently

I've been waking up

as if from death and don't know

what it means—

at the end of days I'll rise again,

or—

sleep slowly turns to death.

Either way, it's not a pleasant feeling.
At the beginning, you
can't fall asleep.
At the end, you
can't wake up.

5.
Another funeral disperses.
Early spring,
and the sun still comes and goes.
Like a father who spanks his small child
and then comforts him,
the Almighty is supposed to comfort us.

But fails.

6.
His death, I think, increased the chances
I'll die the same way.
After all, I'm not different,
and a brain is a brain,
a tumor is a tumor,

and age—age.
If so,
why not me?
On the other hand,
why me?

That is,
of all persons, me?

Of all persons, him.

7.
In the past two weeks, I went
to three funerals,
so I think
I know about funerals—
depressing,
but not terrible.
All the books I'll not read
will remain.
In the coffin, my bones
will recite poetry.
Not the end of the world,
just earth sleep
until further notice.

8. *Without Complaint*

On the Mount of Olives, deep in the ground,

patiently, without complaint,

a little girl, three years old,

waits for her father.

He promised to return

and left her alone.

To work he went.

Hardship and wandering were his lot.

Almost forty years

passed.

Never forgetting, he finally had the time.

He didn't have time to bring a gift.

Just returned:

father to daughter,

dust to dust.

And at the end of days, on the Mount of Olives,

hand in hand they await

the resurrection that will be,

an old man of eighty,

and a child of three.

H. E.

CANCER WARD

1. *Signs and Omens*
A clear morning
and the grass devotes itself to the sun.

Between the white walls of the cancer ward
God reveals Himself
in the dark spot of the lung X-ray
and with signs and omens,
as He did to Pharaoh, hardening his heart.

But we did not harden ours.

2. *Summer Evening at the Convalescent Home*
I lie stretched out on the soft grass
as the sun grows weak.
The body drains itself of thought
like a pool in fall.
And the world—
poplars whisk in the wind.
No more pain or anxiety,
only the grieving gold of leaves
in the wind's grasp.

All my childhood memories
suddenly swish simultaneously
for a moment.
Forever.

3. *Heavy Wings in Deep Darkness*
Unlike Noah
I will not send out a dove.
Now and then I wake
and hear heavy wings in deep darkness.
Between walls I am learning to scream
and not be heard.

The rainbows in the clouds are,
for quite some time,
no answer.

4. *Preparations*
Come evening, prepare for evening.
Move roses to the corridor,
the window open
and the sky covered by clouds
like a face by a newspaper.

All the rest—tick of a clock,
in blank time.

With a rag of light

the morning rubs the stars

from heavens' slate.

If I awake, I'll remember.

5. *Lullaby*

Now to sleep.

If not on the belly,

then on the back.

If not beside a beloved body,

at least thinking about it.

But sleep.

No desire to be first, or second,

only the mattress and me.

And outside,

the sky spreads over the earth

like a mammoth mesh of camouflage.

The Observer above won't see

the heart covered

with its comforters, won't hear

the clicking of the clock,

the craving body.

Just sleep.

6. *Via Dolorosa*
Already not ruler of your body.
Just a crown of thorns and a mouth
covered with the soot of your sighs.
Particularly precise plans: a cross to bear,
a maze of alleyways,
and prayers pierced with nails.
At the end, your body disappears
in the deep darkness
as if stricken from the set.

In the morning flies buzz
in the air, the rumors—
if not resurrection of the dead,
certainly good tidings.

7. *Question*
The pain passes
but the scream remains.
Why?

Why have You forsaken me?
In the green field on the cross
someone surely wondered
whether it was Your doing.

8. *The Third Anniversary*

The cantor scurries on his bicycle.

Someone is always digging

awfully near.

Three years.

The dead doing its thing,

me doing mine,

and the oleander its.

The relatives wait in the designated place.

A merciful God dwells

in the heavens, an airplane passes,

prayers are not heard.

In the dream

I take haven hidden in His wings—

in the dream I'll take haven.

H. E.

JERUSALEM AS SHE IS

1. *Morning*
Morning bends over Jerusalem,
kisses her shoulders,
skims a slender scarf of fog from her thighs,
her sluggish nipples standing out.
Heavy stones form her lips.

And the heart sleeps,
like an *etrog* in its box,
padded with dreams
unknown and unraveled.

A heavy bulldozer
penetrates ancient strata,
revealing memories,
covered with dust and dew.
Even if we don't understand,
we won't ask.

2. *Repairs*
Fix the cracks in the ceiling.
Paint the shutter
green, the door
purple, and the memories

the pale blue of Jerusalem sky.
But the dream will remain broken
like the branch outside your window.

At midnight, midnight prayers,
with all the sighs and groans—
his, mine, yours.

3. *Electric Pole and Sky*
Sometimes I think of Jerusalem
as she looks
from my window in the evening:
a cypress alongside an electric pole and sky,
birds on the wires
like music notes that suddenly sing.
All the rest—
walls, a destroyed Temple, and affliction—
are not in view.
I raise the shutter,
turn the light on,
and a moment later,
off.
Jerusalem
as she is
in the dark of my room.

4. *Snow*

In the end, the snow will cover what time refuses to.

Love will be revealed as a broken tree,

a mouth—a closed sore.

To cry out but not be heard.

A neighborhood without electricity

will sink into deep sleep,

and children tired from roaming

between sets of fairy tales

will stand by the window and look out.

In the garden, unconscious almond trees in white bandages,

and the snow falling very slowly.

It cannot rush.

Like us.

But not heavy like us.

Light.

The bush that froze was

the biblical bush that did not burn

but was consumed.

5. *Changes*

The rain passed,

and the crane was raised again,

like a fist to the sky.

Jerusalem

of changes and us.

And they won't leave

it or us alone.

6. *Mount Scopus*

The sun is like a gold spider,

its body in the sky and its legs

extending to the earth

through the clouds.

From the peak of Mount Scopus,

I look closely at Jerusalem.

The water tanks line the roofs

like flocks of pigeons.

In a tick they'll take off in terror.

The mountain was clipped,

earth was dumped on it,

so now it looks like a mountain

brought from another place.

The olive trees, too, were brought from afar,

but pretend presence here of hundreds of years.

Actually,

not even three.

7. *Jackhammers on the Ninth of Av*
In 70 CE, on the ninth of *Av*,
our Temple was destroyed.
In 1983 CE, on the ninth of *Av*,
the Jerusalem Municipality is paving
a wide street by our house.
For the jackhammers' conductor,
a song.
Such deafening noise
in Titus's head
would surely have silenced the mosquito.
Titus might have preferred the mosquito.
I would have.
Because of our sins then,
we were exiled from our land.
Now, with our sins,
as in exile
we inhabit it.

8. *Dry Bones and Similar Games*
The struggle for survival in Jerusalem
will worsen.
Alongside the turbulent street
palm and other trees were planted—
a war of clean oxygen versus poisonous carbon compounds.

Not far from there,

a war of archeologists

versus *Haredim*—

Please leave the dry bones

until they take shape with skin and sinew.

Not to mention wars between peoples.

Sometimes,

it seems that God

is playing with Jerusalem,

and in jest

shuts a wolf and a sheep

in the same cage

and waits to see what happens.

No wonder people crave

to play similar games.

But when they do,

the carnage is colossal.

9. *On the Old Road*

Eyes closed,

I am on the old road to Jerusalem,

in a taxi.

I spot an orchard by its scent.

In the empty field next to it

rest trucks destroyed in wars.

Should the field become insufficient,

they will chop down the trees around it.

From the shocks,

I recognize train tracks

and the shabby road.

I know without opening my eyes,

like my father in his illness

knew from the pain:

the liver now

and the lungs

and soon the heart.

I sit,

patiently. Soon

I'll arrive.

H. E.

AQUARIUM

1.
Eyes should get used to the dark;
so, too, the heart.
It's not easy, but
at the end of the adjustment
the sights are spectacular.

2.
On one track, the entire evolution is exhibited.
At the beginning, the simplest
conceivable structure:
an internal sac inside an external sac,
the openings serving as a mouth
and anus.

At the end—me,
the crown of perfection,
a clear and complete difference
between mouth (silver tongued)
and anus.
Further development
is inconceivable.

The next stage

is only a return

to the beginning of creation.

3.

After the initial astonishment, the response

is not long in coming.

Nature has strange ideas.

Who could imagine, for example,

an octopus,

or a dog-faced fish,

or a creature that switches sex

in midlife?

Who could imagine

a human being?

4.

In partially lit halls—oceanic depths

and the beginning of time.

The ocean floor

is soft sand

with bright spots, on which a fish

is resting. It is almost impossible

to distinguish it from the surrounding sand.

3.

The sun, setting before my eyes,

will burn out one day.

So, too, my parents' disease,

incurable.

I am tired of thinking.

Like Esau, who gave up his birthright,

I give up love tonight

for sleep.

4.

At the airport—

two medics run with a stretcher.

An old woman has collapsed

on the escalator.

She was lucky it happened here,

where everything is set-up

and ready.

In the place where I stumble,

who will reach out,

who will run

with a stretcher?

H. S.

IN THE CHILDREN'S ROOM

1.

In the children's room

a nightlight

keeps away bad spirits.

In my room

nothing keeps them away.

In the dark

I lie on my back.

The clothes are on the chair,

the scream tucked in my throat,

the closed door

open to nightmares.

2.

Again

a little rabbit with missing limbs

and a teddy bear with worn-out eyes

socialize on the shelf.

I come back to childhood now.

I snip sweet memories,

and put them in my daughter's album.

I swing her high above my life

so she won't know sorrow.

Back and forth I'll carry her

as long as I can.

3.

Again and again I look at my daughter

and ask myself

who does she look like?

Her father? Her mother?

Both?

No one.

4.

It's hard to believe

a nine-year-old child uses

words like *texture* and *quality*.

I don't know what she understands,

what meaning

she assigns them.

I use words like *love* or *life*.

What do I understand?

What do they mean?

5.

In the beginning of summer

the child said:

I saw a tree that belongs to winter.

She meant what she meant.

She didn't mean to draw a picture.

But it came out.

If you add to this

a man who belongs to fall,

a woman who belongs to fears,

and a child of sweet dreams,

you have a family photo.

L. F.-S. and H. S.

HIDDEN LOVE

1. *Growing Up*
The signs of spring
are like bruises
on a boy's body.
He gave up his voice.
Soon
a deeper voice
will force itself
from his throat.
Meanwhile,
his mouth stays shut,
his heart
broken open to love
like an abandoned hut.
Flower buds appeared.
Winter is over and past.

2.
In the garden a bird perches on a stone.
Teach me
the names of the birds
and how to read the map of their wandering.
Show me
the map of your wandering

and the map
of your dwelling
and where I am
in it.

3.
All at once
among those rushing in the street
someone is singing
as if he were someone
else.

All at once
after growing old—
sweet pleasure.

All at once
he fears no evil.

4.
Also signs
of hidden love—
spring and sighs
and pubic hair.
Everywhere,
signs of warning,

and falls

like a branch in a stream.

I'm trying to grasp it.

I'm all mouth,

all thighs;

fireworks in the sky;

a hot spring erupting

from the depths

of the earth.

I'm all sky;

I'm all earth.

8.

The end of summer

at the pool,

one last time

before the end

of the season.

A well-shaped leg,

then the other,

in the cold

water.

The body shivers

and instantly

dozens of tiny tongues

of waves

lick her pubic hair.

9. *Perishable Imperishable*
Elements

that time

can defeat

and those

which it cannot.

Those which it can—

cloth,

paper,

dry autumn leaves,

flowers in a vase,

and love.

Those which it cannot—

clay, steel,

ruins of a temple,

a burden in my heart,

love.

10. *Sukkot at the Seashore*

A sand sea of intermediate days,
a time for sand.
A time for untimely love.
Leaves falling.
Soon the cold.

Thoughts, like birds,
prepare to migrate south,
and we shall prepare
for winter:
We'll count blankets,
check the heating.
And see how the crisscross
lines
spread over the world—
electricity
and water,
planes
and trains.

Undoubtedly
the world is caught
in a huge net;
but we have discovered
a breech.

Perhaps we will still be able

to slip away.

11. *Condemned on the Public Bench*

In the evening

on a public bench

in the center

of a small neighborhood

I wait.

Above the door of the movie house

signs and seasons are changed.

The waving laundry chases low winds

among the bushes,

clouds wander

among stars.

Who would have thought?

But on the bench,

I am condemned

to love

and fall.

L. F.-S. and H. S.

A VISIT TO THE OLD SCHOOL

1. School Breaks
In the school where I studied
the corridors still hum
during breaks
and the smell of oranges lingers;
teachers leave quickly,
on the blackboard—
symbols of chalk;
dust of thoughts.

In a doorway—
a seventeen-year-old girl,
her eyes hold the sadness
of a forty-year-old.

Whatever you do,
you cannot comfort her,
nor can she comfort you.

Too many years.

2. A Lesson in Science
Please sit down.
Today's lesson
deals with fossils.

Look at this huge fern leaf

traced in stone.

Ferns like this don't exist now.

The valley is desolate.

It lacked water.

The whole species vanished.

The human race will also vanish

someday.

In the meantime,

drilling goes on.

The dust of ancient layers is brought up,

remnants of a sea.

Cedar blossoms

are discovered in it.

The climate is changing.

But the mountains react

infinitely slowly.

Rarely can one perceive

the intensity of pain,

as in the great rift valley.

Nevertheless,

ferns of diverse kinds grow

in certain valleys.

This too

will pass, as I explained earlier.

I have nothing to add about this.

Everything passes.

Only the lesson
remains unfinished.

Please, behave accordingly!

3. *A Lesson in the Book of Job*
Boils blossom in the sky of stars;
vapors wander like clouds.
Job takes a potsherd to scrape himself.
Thus he cannot be cured.
Why doesn't he understand?
Luckily, his death might get God in trouble.
But it's ridiculous to claim reparations.
After all, he must become wise.
He has to stop following the moon
when everyone's asleep.
This raises suspicions,
throws shadows. Jackals howl.
He has to understand
there's no meaning to the signs
time writes
on stone,
that the finger of God
draws unintentionally on sand
beside the sea.

He has to consider the pain.
Years pass
until it grows wings
and flies
and is borne on words.
Therefore at times
he cries out.
No doubt
he agitates the frail air
like wind that stirs dry branches
and makes the waters tremble.
On the street people rush
to calm him. They cannot
sleep so long as his voice
is heard. Why doesn't he understand?
After all, he must become wise.
He has to leave the wounds alone.
Otherwise he cannot be cured.

H. S.

SYLLABLES

Twilight of consciousness,
syllables like potsherds,
thick pulp flooding
yellow fields of wheat.

In another place
snow falls
without accumulating.
The wind scatters
sugar powder on a donut.
Dead leaves dance around
a tree, as around
an altar in an ancient rite:
the ceremony of offering
a sacrifice.
The horrible noise
is supposed to cover
the screams of those tied to the altar;
to dull the senses
of those who, this time,
are lucky to watch.

H. S.

THE ERROR

I lean over the page
of calculations:
forty-six lines.
The results
are unreasonable.
Outside the wind
sets dead leaves dancing.
All at once
a man
becomes a picture:
sitting in the middle
of the world and the fall,
leaning over his calculations,
looking for
an error. Around him
dead leaves
dance.
Is this the right time
for calculations?
Soon
it will be dark
and chilly.

But he discovers,

as in the picture,

he cannot

get up.

H. S.

THE EVIL SPIRIT

To cast out the evil spirit
from Saul,
David plays the violin.
I play the violin
to remove the evil spirit
of Saul from me,
the evil spirit
that attacks him
when he recalls
how well David plays.

H. S.

THE PLAGUES

In the *Haggadah*,
as the number of interpretations increases,
so does the number of plagues.

Not only ten
but two hundred,
even two hundred fifty. At once
life becomes a widening web
of plagues.
Everything is clear.
Only I cannot remember them all.
I should, like Rabbi Yehuda,
make signs to remember them.
I do:
Blood, blood and blood.
Alas,
alas
and alas.

H. S.

CHURCH

I walk down the Via Dolorosa

in the opposite direction,

like a film screened in reverse:

descent from the cross,

a third, a second,

and another stumble.

The miracles and sermons

are cancelled, and at the end,

a simple life of manual labor,

an intoxicating scent of wood and sawdust

in a carpentry shop.

H. E.

SEASONAL WIND

Two or three days in a foreign city

have taught you

how rain is punctual.

And the pain:

come three thirty,

it punctures the

left side of the chest.

And death,

like seven doses of sleep,

melts in the mouth

of one who swallows

a soft pastry.

H. E.

REAL LIFE

Let's walk to the lamppost
and back.
The wind touches her face
with a tenderness
she has not known.
This is not real life,
she whispers in the dark.
The sand cradles the sea.
In the distance, the lights—
like jewels displayed
against black.
What is real life?
Work, worry,
fear of want.
Let's walk to the lamppost
and back.
In marriage, she claims,
you are never free.
Nor in love, I infer.
She is divorced
with three children,
abroad on vacation.

The children are with relatives.

Pleasures can be counted

on the fingers

of one hand.

Let's walk to the lamppost

and back.

L. F.-S.

SABBATH EVE

1.

The street empties,

the heart fills

with loneliness.

Sabbath candles

like my mother's fingers

are lit again.

In the newspaper—

a photograph

of the Temple Mount

shot from the Mount of Olives.

In the background—

the mosques.

In the foreground—

cypresses and tombstones

and a caption—

Resurrection

begins here.

2.

On the western slopes

of Jerusalem—

almond trees

like silver candlesticks.

Everything has closed,
but hands
are open for love.

The last preparations
of the body—
perfume, lotion.

In an hour,
in the dark of my room
I will wait for you,
my bride.

L. F.-S.

JET LAG

Three days and three nights,
while without pen, desk, or paper, I recalled
sun in the form of a flaxen-haired girl,
death
in the form of a laborer with a jackhammer
digging ditches
left and right.
Later, I had pen and paper,
but no sun in the form of a girl,
and death suddenly appeared
in the form
of sweet sleep.

H. E.

THE VIEW

In an abandoned village,

a house

falls apart

like a corpse.

Ants go in and out.

From between the tiles,

bushes and grass push

like children

into a courtyard

after class.

Through the demolished roof

the sun gently caresses the walls,

as if they were a nude.

In the window arch,

an almond tree.

A sweet view.

Please don't ask

where the people are.

L. F.-S.

AN EVENING JOG

I circle the stadium, blinded by the light.

The day fades and energy ends.

Animal, vegetable, and mineral demonstrate

peaceful coexistence.

More than that, reconciliation.

As in a hug

grass extends to the track,

which surrounds it like a rim.

A flock of pigeons in aerial drills:

taking off, landing,

twenty pairs of wings

beating the air as one.

But one crow—a lone wolf,

stands

by an empty can,

a commercial

for the end of days.

No need to assume

he is waiting

just for me,

but who knows?

Meanwhile, he is content
with the crust of a sandwich.
What he's got, he's got.
Reason for worry, it seems,
there is not.

L. F.-S.

DIRECTING THE TRAFFIC

Directing the traffic
in the heart
of Tel Aviv,
in the heat
of the afternoon,
at two o'clock
on a hot day,
is the young policewoman's task.
Her movements
replace electrical circuits
that replaced
ancient movements.
Her hips
dance among irises
of smoke and fume.
Her clothes
cling to her body,
the sweat
on her breasts
like sea drops
on the breast of a goddess
rising from the foam.
Ghastly monsters
obey her,

kneel at her feet,

and proceed.

The noise and smoke intensify left and right,

leaving no time to think.

What is needed, of course,

is what she is doing:

directing the traffic.

L. F.-S.

TOUR GUIDE

The tour guide's hand
waves above the crowded group.
All rush to gather around her,
as once upon a time to a flag
on the battlefield:
five shapely fingers
with long fingernails,
painted red.
Imagine them in love.

Because of the rain, my watch stopped,
she apologizes.
It's nothing, madam.
Because of your eyes,
my heart stopped.

H. E.

OVERNIGHT ON THE LAKESHORE

I let time

rock me.

The sea rocks

the empty boats

by the dock,

memories in my eyes

like lights in the water.

A shining strip of light

suddenly looks like

a path

to the moon.

This is the moment.

If you go—

you'll get there.

L. F.-S.

FROM THIS DAY OF YOM KIPPUR
TO THE NEXT

FROM THIS DAY OF YOM KIPPUR TO THE NEXT [1]

I. EVENING

1. *Kol Nidre*
All personal vows
and oaths,
and two little girls
observe your movements
from the women's gallery—

This too is like being observed from above.

With the consent of God
and all present,
with the aid of a few words,
you can
cancel the past,
the future,
a few words
and already all oaths,
worries, dreads
are null and void.

---

[1] In this sequence, about *Yom Kippur* war, there are references to *Yom Kippur* prayers.

2.

By mistake

or not:

The lights are on,

worry at the windows;

how great the deeds,

how deep the thoughts,

from distant borders

to here.

3.

He makes peace,

in His heights meanwhile

air freight from Mahanayim

bears ammunition

and other supplies

to the Golan.

The voice of many waters,

the voice of propellers

and fear—

He is first and last.

4.

He brings on evenings,

opens gates of heaven

the earthly gates

must be

closed

and not opened.

They haven't prepared plans

for escape.

II. MORNING

In the small synagogue

the rabbi and the *hazan* wait

for a *minyan*.

It's doubtful they will come;

meanwhile, the time for morning prayers

passes; youth passes.

In the total silence

only birds can be heard.

The grass reveals top secrets

to the wind

that torments it.

The skies are clear.

The Lord is God.

III. AFTERNOON

1.

At exactly two
the sky falls
with an awful din:
first, second,
seventh heaven.
There is no last.

2.

In Jerusalem
the air is clear.
The stones of houses
are like lizards
basking in the sun.
A yellow butterfly hovers
over purple flowers;
everything quivers with delight.
But the blue sky is misleading:
thunder of airplanes breaking
the sound barrier;
a voice
breaking the barrier
of a scream:
the blue is misleading.

IV. BOMBARDMENT

1.

The shell is in the air.

Without form or body.

In another minute

we may be like that.

Meanwhile, glorified and sanctified

be His great name.

And when all shall cease to be

He alone will reign.

First and last.

2.

So exact is the comparison

and the bombardment:

as glass in the hands of a glazier

who shapes or dissolves it at will.

Surely, He dissolves it.

3.
He formed man with wisdom
and created in him cavities,
hollow and open.
The gunner and driver received
a few more
from a direct blow.

In this way
it is impossible to exist
and stand before You,
healer of all flesh.
Therefore they lie down
hollow and open.

4.
Hear our voices,
hoarse and exhausted.
It's too late to ask
to renew our days as of old
or not to cast us out
in our old age.
Who thinks of old age?
Don't forsake us
if our strength fails;
this may happen
in a few hours.

5.
Our father, our king,

we have no king,

we have no general,

we have no commanding officer

(he died in the bombardment.)

You were supposed to annul

the thoughts of our enemies.

At least annul our own thoughts,

more accurately, our fears;

at any rate, open the gates of heaven.

In the trenches and the pits

we already know we are dust.

Remember this, you too.

We went through fire and water;

we do not claim it was for your Name's sake,

but do it for yourself

if not for us.

As long as the soul is within us;

as long as . . .

6.
A thousand years in your eyes
is like yesterday.
In our eyes
this day of waiting is like a thousand years.
How is it to grow a thousand years older
for one whose life expectancy is seventy years?
The Lord is my refuge,
the shelter is not.
His mercy does not endure forever.
Even a hero cannot be saved
and with all his strength
he will not be delivered.

What we didn't know
was that this time it was
about us.

7.
Moreover,
the one who answered our father Abraham
on Mount Moriah,
who answered Isaac his son when he was bound
on the altar—
doesn't answer now.

V. SUPPORT

At the end of the evening
the *shofar* sounds and the guns thunder.
The heavens open like the Holy Ark.
A pilot and his plane ascend and are swallowed.
The chariot of Israel
and its riders.

VI. DAY BY DAY

1. *Photograph*
In a photograph a soldier is wrapped in a *tallit*.
His face to the photographer,
his back to the setting sun.
The cloud is soaked with blood
even three rationed bandages cannot stop.

2. *Memory*
The grass breaks through
the cracks in the rock.
Far from the place he died
the rumor rustles.
I will not see him again.
I only saw him once,
when by chance he smiled.

In my memory

he will always smile.

3. *Observation Post*

In the binoculars I look for the enemy;

I see antelopes, rare birds,

scarecrows moving in the wind.

Thank God

I don't have to file a report.

4. *Third Watch*

How many more hours must I stand?

The night looks at me like an owl with one eye.

Shaken, I awake and find—

a full moon.

5. *Final Words*

I stand under a metal roof.

Lightning bolts fall around me.

The chance is slim,

but even a bolt can strike my heart.

If this were so,

what would be my

last words?

VII. THE BORDERING RIVER

1.

Already three months—
if not for God,
what are we doing here, going astray
on earth among galaxies growing distant.
What are we?
Something that never happens,
happened.

Who are we
if nobody answers?

2.

Snow covers the mountain tops.
In the mornings I discover in my body
dreams of adolescence like an open wound.
Your love for them is like a bandage,
stinging and healing.
I turn on the radio
and hear an enchanted violin,
hands that are almost mine
play.
My fingers
are covered with forgetfulness.

3.
In the morning on the mountains,
sounds of soldiers coughing
and desert birds.
In the East the sun is like a hot-air balloon,
it's hard to believe that once,
in a matter of seconds,
everything was overthrown here—

Sodom and Gomorrah,
the great rift.

4.
In the evening
I again set my eyes
in the dark.
Sometimes I don't see anything.
Sometimes I see a bush moving
in the wind, hear a piece of scrap rattling,
and the river—a curved metal strip
shining with stars.
I wonder whether time still works
for us, whether it is still working at all?
The people of Israel
live. But the supply-keeper's assistant
died from a car accident.
Not a heroic death,

no "May God avenge his blood."
But then who will take vengeance
against whom, I ask,
and for how long
shall the people of Israel live?

5.
A soldier stands at an intersection.
He is graying,
his thumb raised;
when will he rest?

Twenty-four-hours leave
cannot compensate for war.
When he arrives, his wife will run
barefoot to him—
his heart will leap to her
as far as a heavy heart can,
in a heavy body
desperate for sleep.

6.
The final evening.
The River Jordan returns to its size
and we to ours.
Not a chosen people,

only a prolonged disease in the world,

longings that cannot be pacified,

ultimately just like everybody else.

Time vomits us out from its midst

like dead fish on the river's bank.

Tomorrow we will say

see you soon,

but not here.

If not here,

where?

VIII. TRAINING

1. *Death Rehearsal*

In the drill I am one of the fallen.

I was wounded (apparently by a shell).

They identify me (two who know me personally).

They carry me to the collection point,

gather my belongings (rifle, watch,

wallet with a family photo).

The doctor confirms my death.

Everyone signs the appropriate form.

For the sake of pretense
we laugh out loud—

but everyone knows.

2. *Evacuating the Injured*
You and you and you,
run with the stretcher.

Be sure the backpack
has all the first-aid items:
bandage; tourniquet.
Also:
don't expect the soldier
to have his personal bandage,
to tell you where he is wounded—

to breathe.

3. *Rebuke*
They might give way on many things
but not on this:
not knowing where the injured are,
who is dead,
who is alive.

It's not so smart

for those not involved,

to read a newspaper,

or chat with a neighbor.

In another minute

they'll have to run with stretchers

and they won't know how.

4. *Fortified Targets*

At the entrance to the trench

I am supposed to imagine an enemy soldier

and to fight him.

I empty the cartridge, screaming,

to avoid hearing his scream.

He who ran behind me

now runs in front of me. At the curve

I take the lead until

the target is cleared, I pronounce.

At the end of the trench

stands the new commander,

and declares it a poor performance.

Start over from the beginning!

The previous commander

died in the war's first moment

from a direct hit—

a perfect performance.

5. *Dog Tags*

You can't overemphasize the importance of tags.

When the face is destroyed or the body

burned—it's possible

to identify the soldier this way.

Indeed, there's the case

of a unit that operates

at the rear of the enemy

and can be totally

wiped out.

Therefore, the little note

the soldier leaves

with the officer

at the time of takeoff.

When needed

it will testify.

6. *Evaluating the Situation*

You must evaluate the situation
continuously!
It's hard, in battle
there are always surprises.
Only this is certain:
In the dark one is more afraid
than in the light,
and the one who will survive
will also recount—
a hero,
perhaps he can evaluate
the situation.

7. *Briefing*

It's all right for now, the officer explains,
his stick under his arm,
his rank on his shoulders,
all right for now.
By this he means everything can change
in a moment:
Now we are here
under the cool shade of the shed,
in a second,
when the bomb falls—
God will reveal Himself in a cloud
and in the fog of war.
For now.

IX. TERRITORIES

1. *Reconnaissance*
Far from my home
I see how summer
makes the stubborn grass die
but cannot overcome
my love.
Dreams are still
our real home.
Before me
strips of soft sand,
orchards.
Across from one of the barriers
an enemy,
perhaps in ambush,
perhaps not.
I count the hours left
until I return to you,
to count the hours left
until I return
here.
Territories
and more territories.

2. *Rest*

When I lie down on the ground

I discover

a colony of snails

on a green stalk of thistle.

So many forms of being,

and this is mine.

Again they hustle me.

—Just a minute,

just another minute,

I promise I'll get up,

promise to keep going.

3. *Duty Roster*

Watches for pillows

of those who sleep

measure the remaining time

and the nightmare.

Stones for pillows

made soft dreams for Jacob,

angels going up and down.

For me—hard dreams,

soldiers in a pup tent,

the sky falling like a ceiling

into restless sleep:

Get up, now—

it's your turn.

X. *MUSAF* (Additional Service)

1.

We are guilty.

We have lied.

We have strayed.

We must always ask forgiveness,

you know:

all that is hidden,

all that is revealed.

2.

God supports all who have fallen.

It is doubtful whether this is true

for those who lie

in puddles of their blood

outside their posts—

perhaps in the end of days,

in the framework

of the general resurrection

of the dead.

3.

In those days,

on the day of the Sabbath—

two innocent yearling lambs.

In this time,

on the day of *Yom Kippur*—

two thousand five hundred

and twenty-seven

men.

XI. *NE'ILA* (Concluding Service)

Open the gate for us

even as it closes,

I mumble, but I know

the gate is already closed

and locked.

In the *Mahzor*

I borrowed from my neighbor—

mine was lost in the war—

are dates of births

and deaths,

so as not to forget,

so as not to remember.

In a little while

the swaying of the body in prayer

will cease

and the swaying will return to the bushes,

the grass.

By the door—

drimias, like *Yahrzeit* candles,

will shiver in the wind.

L. F.-S. and H. S.

THE MELODY LINGERS

1985 — VISIT

1.

All the roads lead to Auschwitz.

All the roads

in the sky and on the ground.

Whether you like it

or not.

2.

One thousand nine hundred eighty

and five more.

Forty years have passed.

And yet, come night,

winds still gust scents of dust and ash.

3.

Of all the words in the dictionary,

the curators chose museum.

So to speak,

on exhibit here are all

the horrors that human monsters

could conceive.

4.

And four years later,

one thousand nine hundred and eighty-nine,

a sign reads:

HERE FOUR MILLION POLES

FOUND THEIR DEATH.

The curators,

by chance only,

forgot to write—

all of Polish Jewry.

5.

The photo shows

a father and his three-year-old daughter

in his arms, tucked tight to his heart.

From behind, the soldier aims his weapon.

She will never know

the meaning of that hug,

ever.

The soldier behind, the photographer on the side.

Time,

which never stops,

froze this instant in the photo.

Forever father.

Forever daughter.

6.

From 7 October 1941 to 1 March 1942 fenced and separate blocks (numbers 1-3, 12-14, 22-24) housed a work camp containing Russian prisoners of war. Some ten thousand men were registered in the camp. Legions of POWs died from starvation, grueling work, and particularly cruel treatment at the hands of the SS. Some were gassed with Zyklon B. They were executed by special order of the Gestapo heads. Prisoners of war who refused to work when it was freezing outside were taken, naked, from the blocks, and camp guards poured water on them, causing many to die. In a five-month period, nine hundred thousand prisoners of war were murdered. About one thousand Soviet prisoners of war who survived were transferred, in March 1942, to Birkenau, a camp then under construction.

7.

After a successful prison break by Polish prisoners, the German police on occasion arrested the escapees' relatives and sent them to the camp as a warning to others. They were housed here, under a sign indicating that they will remain in the camp until the escaped prisoner is captured.

8.

At the entrance to the camp stands the infamous sign,

Work sets you free,

to delude anyone

who still has illusions.

9.

ONE OF THE TOUGHEST MOMENTS OF LIFE IN THE CAMP WAS ROLL CALL. AT FIRST, THEY GATHERED THE PRISONERS IN THE MAIN SQUARE, AND AFTER THE NEW BUILDINGS WERE BUILT, THEY STOOD THE PRISONERS ALONG THE CAMP'S ROADS, IN FRONT OF THE BLOCKS. THOUSANDS OF PRISONERS WERE FORCED TO APPEAR FOR ROLL CALL, WHICH LASTED FOR HOURS ON END.

10.

I AM KEEPING READY MY DEATH'S-HEAD UNITS TO KILL MEN, WOMEN, AND CHILDREN OF POLISH BIRTH AND POLISH TONGUE WITHOUT PITY OR MERCY. POLAND WILL BE DEPOPULATED AND GERMANS WILL SETTLE THERE.

11.

FOR THE CONTEMPORARY WORLD AUSCHWITZ IS THE SYMBOL OF HOLOCAUST—THE MASS EXTERMINATION OF THE JEWISH NATION. HOWEVER, BEFORE THE FIRST TRANSPORTS OF THE JEWS TO THE GAS CHAMBERS, THOUSANDS OF POLES AS WELL AS OTHER NATIONS' REPRESENTATIVES WERE KILLED IN THE CAMP.

12.

True.

But we did not request birthright.

Moreover,

we were ready

to forgo it in exchange

for lentil broth,

like Esau did in his time.

The problem: no offer was made.

13.

In the year one hundred and twenty by Christian count—

ten Jewish sages were killed by Roman rule.

At the end of the year nineteen hundred and forty

and another five as they count the years—

thousand times six thousand.

14.

Auschwitz—the valley of death.

The most evil place in our world.

To be precise, in all possible worlds.

Remember everything that happened here.

Remember and retell—

to your sons and daughters,

generation to generation, forever.

H. E.

IS THIS OLD AGE?

1.

From the window I watch the sun set

in thousands of colors.

Another day has gone by.

The questions have remained unanswered.

Come evening, what shall I say?

Apparently, I'm a parable

without a moral.

2.

In the stadium of my thoughts I run,

picking up my pace.

The Almighty, you might say, measures time for me.

and the stands are empty.

Nobody to cheer me on.

Only me

thinking to myself.

3.

When I was a child, in the evenings,

I wandered around outside—a street child,

playing war, knights, and lovers.

At supper time

my mother, at the balcony, called out:

Come and eat!

Throughout the world, her voice was heard.

I still dream of hearing her call.

And loudly I respond:

I'm coming.

4.

All the world's a stage

and all the men and women merely players.

Time dictates precise rules for acting.

It is meticulous,

it is merciless.

I always listened to it,

I obeyed,

I acted:

I was child, youth, adult,

soldier, and lover.

I was son, I was father,

and now—grandfather.

Only at times, when not in role,

facing the mirror, amazed I

stand and look: in fact,

who am I?

5.

Days are coming,

the object will be cut off from its name,

the name from its object.

And the days have come.

And I am old.

And where to now?

6.

In my memory's huge cellar

I look for one forgotten detail.

If lucky,

I'll find it instantly.

If not,

I'll have to check piece by piece.

I'm not complaining.

There's time,

there's patience,

but, alas, there's no one to ask.

7.

On Hudson River's shore, the generations change,

and they still run:

young boys and girls, women,

baby-carriage pushers, old folk,

the disabled in electric scooters, and me too,

from behind,

struggling to keep up, to keep

my place.

A statuesque girl, her legs exposed

to her crotch, passes me,

raising in me an old desire.

So I pick up speed,

but give up a minute later.

8. *In Therapy*

"What bothers you?"

the therapist asks.

"I'm afraid,"

I reply.

"Of what?"

"Of old age, of course,

but mainly of sleep."

"This is not surprising.

Sleep is like death. Death is

dreamless sleep."

"So what do you suggest?"

"Very simple. Count!

To one hundred at least."

"And if that doesn't help?"

"Keep counting.

Numbers, as you know,

are countless."

9.

Recently I've had weird dreams.

I get up in the morning looking for answers,

like the king of Egypt many years ago.

For him, Joseph interpreted.

But now—

who will interpret for me?

10.

At midnight, I too,

like that girl in the fairytale,

delay my death

by telling stories.

To myself.

But without robbers

or magic lantern.

Only my childhood,

my father, my mother,

on a balcony of a house,

in the shade of the pines.

11.
Seemingly, everything is like it once was.
In fact, all has changed.
Mainly the pace.
The movement's pace.
Like in the cinema, a past event
is screened in slow motion.
I behave the same way:
wake up slowly, sit up, stand up,
go to the table.
The time—like a literature teacher dictating
the topic of an essay to his pupils.
And I, the obedient pupil, write—
in slow motion.

12.
Once everything was clear as can be:
the houses, the roads, the trains, the planes.
Now nothing is understood:
not people, not words, not language, not love,
not life.

13.
And at the end of it all—
in the cemetery,
we all are a hyphen
stuck between two dates.

14.

Night has descended.

In a small neighborhood, down the slope

of a street,

hand in hand go

a grandfather and his granddaughter.

He is the end,

she is the beginning.

And God saw

that it was very good.

H. E.

THE MELODY LINGERS

Tonight—
like every night.
I lie on my bed,
longing for sleep to come.
I count sheep,
one and one more.
I've already reached one hundred,
but nothing happened.
again and again, I call the melody.
Nothing happens.

The melody lingers.

S. V.

A CHILD WITH SPECIAL NEEDS

In memory of my brother, Uri (1940-2013)

1.

Alongside his sickbed I sit.

His eyes, window to the soul,

say now—

the pain is insufferable.

And soon they'll go dark.

You were and are no longer.

I, too, once was,

and before long,

I'll be no more.

2.

A child with special needs died.

A child he remained, in old age as well.

Ended is his suffering,

which from childhood to his bad old age

spread like cancer in his soul.

Intolerable pain he bore,

like an ant,

who drags and drags and drags a grain of wheat

much heavier than she

to her nest—

a hole in the ground that swallows her whole.

So, too, his death—

a wide-open pit being covered by stacks of soil.

H. E.

ON THE TWENTY-FIRST OF TISHREI [2]

The twenty-first of the month of *Tishrei*—
God was taken from the Ark on that day,
borne on the shoulders of those who bear him,
like a soccer star from the stadium.
In front of the empty Ark
stood children two, three, four years old,
with eyes of blue and hair of gold.
No other angels made their mark
by the open Ark on that day,
the twenty-first of *Tishrei*.

H. E.

---

[2] The day Jews celebrate the holiday of *Simchat Torah* (Rejoicing with the Torah).

THE SUN AT ITS PEAK

A spring morning—
the cypress stretching tall and the sun at its peak,
and a helicopter in the sky
sketching circles,
like a child in art class, announcing:
everything's okay.
Welcome a lovely day.

                                                    H. E.

I HEAR

I hear chirping and think
bird, I hear howling and think
jackal,
I see you and think
love,
and almost instantly—also serenity.
A word for every thing.
Wonders of the language.

H. E.

NAVIGATION

While you looked at the map

I looked at the world.

With the aid of words, we passed from things' names

to the things themselves:

houses and churches, parks, and also a lake.

On and on, till last light,

in which we remained.

H. E.

NIGHT THOUGHTS

1. *Forecast*
Death is like an ongoing tone
of a station
at broadcasts' end.

Rain outside
and tomorrow's forecast—
the same.

I testify in writing
on this life—
only I can testify—

that it is running out.
What am I to do?

And tomorrow's forecast—
the same.

2. *Coat*
Under the awful fatigue and headache and lack of sleep
death is folded like a coat
my mother laid in the bottom of the bag
for the field trip.

At night, when it's chilly,

spread it out and cover yourself.

It will warm you.

3. *Let the Blood Flow*

Sleep is like a down payment

on death, or perhaps

just pretends to be.

Turned over on the page where I stopped,

I lay down the book from my hand,

and my life.

A childhood memory

momentarily spreads like a hand fan.

To get the blood to flow

freely,

I draw my arm from under my beloved's head back to me.

Be it now or tomorrow,

if people discover us in this position,

they'll even imagine

serenity.

H. E.

SLEEPING PROBLEMS

1.

The moment comes that
time stands still. Need to
give it a push.
More than that,
need to move it, to oust spirits, demons.
I read a book, write
words.

If I had somewhere to go,
I'd go.

2.

How much time is left,
I ask, and with incredible intellectual effort,
like in the ancient text,
I respond to myself, first half of
the time and then half of
the half of the time:
that's a half plus a quarter,
and then an eighth,
and so forth and so on
forever.
Oh, what pleasure
sweet sleep will bring.

3.
How Rahn died suddenly
I saw, by chance, in the morning paper.

Just died,
and at his age. No
omen of troubles and no
sign. And no history.
Who else might
suffer the same fate?
Must every day see someone
take leave of everything?

—Every day.
Nevertheless, I
request only a day,
just one day

that does not.

4.
On second thought, I
raise my first thought.
If I remain wakeful,
I'll reach a seventh and eighth thought.

I anticipate a turn
albeit in vain.
Better is a walk for digestion's sake,
and to relieve a bothersome backache.

Thus, of all the thoughts in the world,
digestion and the back problem stand out.

If this becomes known, it may harm my image.

So, on second thought,
I fervently hope the first thought ceases to exist.
Indeed, that all the thoughts cease to exist.

I'm frightened.

So, alternatively, please,
sleep for a limited time.

H. E.

PICTURES AT AN EXHIBITION—THE MUSEUM OF MODERN ART

1.

A huge red rectangle divided into

three unequal sections

by vertical lines.

The curator implores me to look, think deeply,

and be impressed profoundly.

2.

And then—the abstract room.

I am asked to do

drills in abstraction.

This is a flower after the abstraction.

This is the woman in nude depiction.

But with all due respect

to the artist,

please show me how to return

to the original.

H. E.

IN HIS HAND

In His hand, I commit my spirit.
In the barber's hands, my hair.
To the masseur, my body.
If so, what is left there
for me?

H. E.

THE TASTE OF LIFE

At the airport's departing-flights waiting area,
hundreds of people.
On gigantic screens advertisements telling
of the taste of life to all who think it interesting.
For those who don't know,
Coke in a glass bottle.
What a relief though.
Now, finally, we know
what the taste of life is.
But what
is the meaning?

H. E.

PLAYGROUND

1.
On the swings at the playground
the generations change.
Those who were once children
are now fathers.
The swing goes up and goes down,
a pendulum of generations.

2.
What are you doing there?
A father gets anxious.
Get off the ladder, now.
It's dangerous!
Who allowed you?
Once, I too climbed
without permission.
Now I simply
don't climb.

3.
Two-year-old Asaf
still cannot,

so he sits in the sandbox

with bucket and shovel

and builds a tall tower.

H. E.

BIRTHDAY SONG

For Shoshi Hyman

Birthday.

God's small gifts.

Early morning, get up and go

to saunter backstreets now empty.

The world is disrupted,

incurably so.

The birds have migrated, and the tree by the fence,

in utter pining, is losing its leaves.

What was hoped to be is not.

Winter is not winter,

peace is not peace,

and Jerusalem is not Jerusalem.

But love is love.

It forgives the body its treasons

and patiently waits.

The thoughts that change childhood

from bitter to sweet

are the zest of maturity.

Time, you might say, a long-distance runner,

is leaving us behind.

And like one retired from competition,

we return to where we went astray,

and start anew:

Birthday.

H. E.

ON HUDSON RIVER'S BANK

On Hudson River's bank the joggers, panting,
energy expending,
hopefully their youth retaining.
But still we see several remaining
at the rear.

On one of the doors, a sign:
Please wait! I'll return soon.

H. E.

THE LAST QUARTET

The last movement. With supreme effort

the composer stoops over the score sheet:

The hard decision;[3]

presumably, because these were years of poverty,

poor esteem, despised loves,

not to mention illnesses and hearing loss.

Now, last words

to himself and to all future generations,

and the sudden insight that it must be.

In his eyes now

the light of hidden worlds,

and thus, defiantly he ends,

with a complete surprise,

in a major key.

S. V.

---

[3] At the beginning of the last movement of his last quartet, Opus 135, Beethoven wrote (in German): "The hard decision. Must it be?" And immediately afterwards: "it must be," and finished the quartet in a major key.

THE MELODY REMAINS

1. Surely the Thing is Known
My young daughter too already realizes
that I'll die one day.

Surely the thing is known.

Now, like Moses in Egypt,
I'll have to flee to the desert
and seek substitute modes of being,
in the dust, in the wind.
In words.

2. Gifts
Deep in slumber, my daughter hugs
her dolls:
a gift from Daddy, a gift from Mommy,
a gift from Grandpa,
of blessed memory.
In the second room, I
strive to overcome my fear,
try calming thoughts,
memories:

a gift from Daddy, a gift from Mommy,

a gift from Grandpa,

of blessed memory all.

3. *Memory of Others*

I've already forgotten,

but my daughter remembers how,

when she was two years old,

I carried her on my shoulders and sang

"The Little Rabbit."

So it is,

erased from my memory,

I become a memory of others.

So it is,

despite everything,

continuation.

4. *Two Voices*

Autumn eve in a park.

Half the world is awake

and half is asleep.

Sleep as temporary death,

wakefulness

as temporary eternity,

alternately.

On the sun's last rays

children slide

and ascend again to the tower top.

Suddenly, on the bench, the moment is

like a thousand years.

In two voices I sing with my daughter:

The days pass,

a year goes by.

Two voices.

The melody remains.

H. E.

DEPARTURE

> *When you are young you say Song of Songs and when you are old you say Ecclesiastes.*
> Pirkei Avot

The time to depart is here.
All was known already
from the Book of Genesis.
I'm not complaining.
In fact, I've been lucky.
I made it to old age in good health,
my mind still clear.
But I have no choice—I must depart.

At the very last minute I recall
the ancient wise man who, about to die,
ordered a sacrifice to the god of health.
I never grasped his intent.
Was he giving thanks for the health he had,
or for being cured of the malady of life?

So, farewell my loved ones.
This time, sad to say and to my dismay,
we'll not meet again on this, or any, day.

H. E.

The Poet

Shlomo Vinner was born in 1937, and raised in Jerusalem. After earning a PhD in Mathematics at the Hebrew University of Jerusalem, he switched to Mathematics Education, pursuing post-doctoral studies in the United States, during which time he met the poet Howard Schwartz, who became his first translator.

Vinner returned to Israel and taught at the Hebrew University of Jerusalem and Ben-Gurion University of the Negev.

Vinner began writing poetry at the age of twenty-two. His books of poems in Hebrew include *For a Few Hours Only* (1972); *Tremor and Earth* (1986), which was awarded an ACUM (Association of Composers and Writers in Israel) prize; *Suddenly Life* (1992), supported by a Jerusalem Foundation for Literature grant; *Until the Sun and the Light will Darken* (2014), and *Roads* (2019), both published with the support of ACUM's Social and Cultural Fund.

In 1991, a book of English translations of his poems, *Jerusalem as She Is*, was published by BkMk Press, of the College of Art and Sciences, University of Missouri, Kansas City. His work also appears in Hebrew-poetry anthologies and in French and Italian anthologies.

His book on mathematics education, *Mathematics, Education and Other Endangered Species*, was published by Springer in 2019.

The Translators

Howard Schwartz's most recent books are *The Library of Dreams: New & Selected Poems, 1965-2013* and *A Palace of Pearls: The Stories of Rabbi Nachman of Bratslav.*
www.howardschwartz.com

Laya Firestone-Seghi is a psychotherapist in Hollywood, FL. Besides Shlomo Vinner, her translations from Hebrew include poets Yehuda Amichai, Gabriel Preil and Natan Zach.
www.layaseghi.com

Harold Ellason, who grew up on the Jersey Shore and has lived in Israel for almost fifty years, began translating poetry five years ago. *The Melody Lingers* is the first publication containing his poetic translations.

Recent Books from Singing Bone Press

A Hermit Has No Plural by Gabor Gyukic

My God, How Many Mistakes I've Made by Endre Kukorelly (translated from Hungarian by Gabor Gyukic and Michael Castro)

How Things Stack Up by Michael Castro

Two Gardens: Modern Hebrew Poems of the Bible (Poems by twenty-four Israeli poets translated by Jeff Friedman and Nati Zohar)

Poems from the Buddha's Footprint by Sunthorn Phu (translated from Thai by Noh Anothai)

Double Identity by Allison Joseph

Doubled Radiance: Poetry and Prose of Li Qingzhao (translated from Chinese by Karen An-Hwei Lee)

We Need to Talk: New and Selected Poems by Michael Castro

The Heart Attacks of the Soul: Gypsy Cantos by Attila Balogh (translated from Hungarian by Gabor Gyukic and Michael Castro)

Butter in a Jar: Days in the Life of Iola Thomas by Jerred Metz

Uncle Duke Gathers His Wits: Truths and Heresies by W. K. Haydon

The Angel of Mons: A World War I Legend by Jerred Metz

www.ingramcontent.com/pod-product-compliance
Lightning Source LLC
Chambersburg PA
CBHW061653040426
42446CB00010B/1713